ONE STEP ABOVE

The Invisible Ceiling That Shapes Ambition, Identity, & Growth

Reginald A. Calloway

www.AboveTheoryMedia.com

One Step Above

Reginald A. Calloway

Published by

Above Theory Media

www.AboveTheoryMedia.com

Book Production by

TrueVinePublishing.org

Printed in the United States of America—First printing.

ACKNOWLEDGMENTS

This book belongs to more than one voice.

First and foremost, to **Jennifer Bass**. For over a decade, she heard about this book long before it existed. She listened to the theories, the questions, the late-night connections, the unfinished thoughts. She didn't need them to be polished to recognize their value. When I didn't know how to write, she listened. When I didn't know how to structure, she remembered. When I doubted whether this belonged anywhere outside my head, she never did.

This book exists because she held space for it before it had form. To the people who listened when these ideas were still rough, who asked questions, pushed back, and allowed me to test thoughts out loud, thank you.

Some of you know exactly who you are. Your presence mattered more than you know.

To my family—complex, layered, and deeply formative—you are part of this story whether named or not. Much of what's written here comes from living inside those dynamics, learning from them, and carrying their lessons forward with care.

And finally, to the reader. If something in these pages feels familiar, that's not a coincidence.

It means you've been standing near a ceiling of your own.

AUTHOR'S NOTE

This book didn't begin on paper. It began in conversations.

For years, I carried these ideas in my head, talking them out, testing them, revisiting them, refining them without ever writing them down. I didn't lack thoughts. I lacked a way to place them where they could live.

So instead of writing, I spoke. I spoke to the people closest to me. I spoke in fragments, theories, stories, and questions. I circled the same ideas again and again, not knowing they were forming a framework, only knowing they felt true.

What you're holding now is not something I suddenly decided to write. It's something I finally learned how to translate. Over time, a pattern kept revealing itself. I watched intelligent, capable people stall, not because they lacked talent or opportunity, but because they encountered an invisible limit they couldn't name. Growth seemed to slow not at failure, but at a certain level of relative success.

Being one step above felt like progress until it quietly became a ceiling.

The structure of this book is intentional. The early chapters focus on identifying patterns, where the One Step Above mindset shows up and how it shapes ambition, identity, and growth across families, friendships, education, and work. These chapters are not meant to accuse or diagnose. They are meant to help you recognize something that often operates subconsciously.

The later chapters shift from recognition to response. They explore ways to move beyond this ceiling: how to grow without burning bridges, how to leave familiar rooms without resentment, and how to become comfortable being a beginner again.

This book isn't here to shame anyone. It's here to identify a pattern.

This pattern shows up:

♦ in families
♦ in friendships
♦ in education
♦ in entrepreneurship
♦ in everyday life
♦ in wealth
♦ in identity

It helps explain why so many capable people stop climbing. It's not because they can't go higher, but because going higher would require letting go of who they are around others.

This book names the pattern first, then offers a way through it. If you see yourself in these pages, that isn't an accident. This book isn't here to tell you who to be. It's here to help you see where you may have stopped and why.

PREFACE

I didn't set out to write a book about limits. I set out to understand why growth felt harder than it should. For a long time, I believed the struggle was external: a lack of resources, access, and opportunity. But the more I watched people grow (and stop growing), the clearer it became that something internal was often at work.

Not fear exactly. Not laziness. Not ignorance. Identity.

People didn't stop because they couldn't go further; they stopped because going further would require becoming unfamiliar, letting go of the version of themselves that finally felt safe, respected, or "enough."

That moment when relative success replaces expansive vision is what this book is about. This is not a book about blame. It's not about class versus wealth, intelligence versus ignorance, or right versus wrong. It's about how comparison quietly replaces curiosity, how familiarity disguises itself as humility, and how love, loyalty, and belonging can become invisible limits.

I've lived on both sides of this ceiling. I've stayed too long in rooms that no longer fit. I've shrunk myself to keep the peace. I've avoided being a beginner because I didn't want to feel small again. And I've also learned—slowly and imperfectly—how to step beyond those limits without burning my life down in the process.

This book doesn't promise dramatic exits or overnight transformation. It offers something quieter and more sustainable: clarity. Read it slowly. Notice what makes you uncomfortable. Pay attention to the chapters that feel personal. Those are usually the ceilings worth examining.

TABLE OF CONTENTS

The Invisible Ladder

"The most dangerous prison isn't the one that keeps you from rising. It's the one that convinces you you've already risen enough."

—Reginald A. Calloway

Most people don't want to be rich; far from it, even. Many people don't have a sick craving for power, either. The only desire in people's lives isn't just to be free. They desire to be **one step above** those who surround them in the ocean we call life.

That phrase is uncomfortable. It sounds wrong to assume we are sharks in life, but once you see it, you can't unsee it.

The Ladder Nobody Talks About

From the outside, life looks like a straight climb:

- ♦ poverty to stability
- ♦ stability to comfort
- ♦ comfort to wealth

But that's not how most successful individuals move. What really exists is an **invisible ladder: one** step up at a time, measured not by potential, but by **comparison**.

People don't ask, "How far can I go?"

They ask:

"Who am I ahead of?"

That question quietly shapes choices, relationships, ambition, and identity. It also builds a prison without bars.

A prison of comfort.

Why One Step Feels Safe

Being one step above gives you something powerful. Undeniability:

- dignity without responsibility
- confidence without the fear of risk
- superiority without transformation

You don't have to change too much. Contentment is a premium.

You don't have to feel stupid. You're the smartest in the room.

You don't have to sit in rooms where you don't belong *yet*.

You get to teach instead of learn. Judge instead of adapting. Explain instead of listening, and most importantly, you get to stay familiar.

The Prison Nobody Recognizes

Here's the truth:

The One Step Above mindset doesn't feel like a limitation. It is meant to be far more than that. A step taken is an **achievement**. A resounding victory.

The man with a job lectures men without one.

The person who reads a little mocks those who cannot.

The family with a house looks down on families with an apartment.

The entrepreneur with a small business lectures the man with the job on the power of self-employment.

There is also a flipside. This One-Step-Above mentality also becomes a prison.

The man with a job, avoids the entrepreneur

The entrepreneur with a small business avoids partnering with larger businesses.

Each person feels successful. Each person feels superior, so they run from situations that will make them feel inferior. Each person has unknowingly locked their own ceiling. Their own potential. A ceiling where they avoid looking further into that said potential.

It's not about intelligence

This prison has nothing to do with intelligence. That is far beyond the point. Some of the smartest people you'll ever meet are trapped inside it. Success is an avenue that looks different for most people. This prison is the clearest expression of the differences among successful individuals.

Intelligence doesn't free you from identity. It often **strengthens it**. If being "the smart one" is how you survive, you will unconsciously avoid rooms where you're not. If being "the one who made it out" defines you, you will resist environments that make you ordinary again.

Growth requires becoming a beginner again. The One Step Above prison makes that feel like a loss.

The Subconscious Contract

Most people never consciously choose this. They enter into a silent agreement with their environment:

I won't outgrow you too fast.

You won't make me question my life.

That agreement feels like loyalty. It feels like humility. It feels like belonging. But it comes with a price.

Once you are one step above:

- Moving two steps up feels unnecessary
- Taking five steps up feels threatening
- Going ten steps up feels impossible

Not because it is, but because **your identity can't yet survive it.**

So you stall. You rationalize. You explain it away.

"I don't need all that."

"I'm just trying to be normal."

"I don't want to change."

Those sentences sound peaceful, but they are often fear in disguise.

ASK YOURSELF

If nobody around you could see your success, how far would you really want to go?

That answer tells you where your ceiling is.

Where the Ceiling Begins

"The first ceiling you ever meet doesn't look like a limitation. It looks like home."

–Reginald A. Calloway

Childhood and Environment

No one wakes up one day and decides to limit themselves. If that were the case, there would never be anyone who chooses this step over. The ceiling is installed **before choice ever feels like choice**.

Before ambition, before fear, before language, there is **environment**.

Your first classroom isn't school. It's the living room. The block. The dinner table. The people you hear talking when they don't think you're listening. That's where the One Step Above mindset begins.

Not as a belief, but as a **reference point that becomes a turning point**.

How "Winning" Gets Defined Early

Every environment has its own definition of success.

In some places:

- Success is safety, where familiarity combines.
- Success is survival, where challenges never arise.
- Success is not being the worst-off person in the room; it is the most successful one.

So children don't learn to ask: "What's possible?" They learn to ask: "How do I not fall to the bottom? How do I ensure I won't fail?

That's the first rung of the invisible ladder, and once you step on it, everything above it is measured relative to it, not absolutely.

The Quiet Lesson Children Absorb

Children don't need lectures to learn ceilings. They watch reactions.

They notice:

- Who gets praised
- Who gets corrected
- Who gets warned
- Who gets laughed at

They learn very quickly:

- Curiosity can be dangerous
- Confidence can be punished
- The difference can cost belonging

So they adjust. Not consciously. Instinctively.

When Comparison Replaces Vision

In environments shaped by scarcity, comparison becomes a matter of survival.

Someone is always:

- a little smarter
- a little poorer
- a little worse off

Being one step above feels like stability. So instead of imagining an open horizon, children learn to scan the room.

Who am I better than? Who am I worse than?

That becomes the internal compass. Not direction, but **position**.

Why Intelligence Gets Misread

This is where intelligence often gets misunderstood. In many environments, intelligence isn't rewarded for expansion. It's tolerated only if it:

- ◆ doesn't disrupt hierarchy
- ◆ doesn't challenge elders
- ◆ doesn't create distance

So a child who asks too many questions gets labeled:

- ◆ difficult
- ◆ arrogant
- ◆ slow
- ◆ unfocused

Not because they are, but because their curiosity threatens the ceiling.

The Role of Shame

Shame is the tool that keeps the ladder in tact. Not a loud shame. A quiet shame. The kind that says:

- "Don't do too much."
- "Don't embarrass us."
- "Don't forget who you are."

Over time, children internalize this. They don't need enforcement anymore. They enforce it on themselves.

How the Ceiling Feels Normal

The most dangerous part of early ceilings is that they feel *natural*.

Children don't know:

- What they're missing
- What else exists
- How far could they go

They only know what's modeled. So when later opportunities appear: education, travel, wealth, new ideas, they feel foreign, and foreign often feels unsafe.

Why Leaving Feels Like Betrayal

When someone from that environment begins to grow, it disrupts the shared reality, leaving the other people in that environment feeling betrayed.

Another person's growth and achievement suggest:

"There was more room than we thought."

That implication is threatening. So the environment responds, not with arguments, but with emotion:

Guilt.

Mockery.

Withdrawal.

The ceiling tightens.

The Pattern Repeats

What starts in childhood follows people into:

- friendships
- relationships
- careers
- families
- leadership

The ladder never disappears. It just changes rooms.

ASK YOURSELF

What did my environment reward? What did it quietly discourage?

Education, Intelligence, and the Illusion of Being Smart

"The most dangerous level of intelligence is the one that feels superior without ever being challenged."

—Reginald A. Calloway

One of the most damaging lies people carry isn't that they're stupid. It's that they're **smart enough**.

Smart enough to survive.

Smart enough to explain.

Smart enough to stay one step above.

And that illusion quietly replaces mastery.

How Intelligence Gets Redefined

In many environments, intelligence isn't measured by depth. It's measured by **comparison to those surrounding us**.

If you can read better than someone who can't read at all, you're "smart." If you can do basic math while others can't, you're "good with numbers." If you can explain things verbally, you're "intelligent."

But no one asks:

"How far can this go?"

They ask:

"Who am I better than?"

That's where education stops being a ladder and becomes a fence. A fence halting growth.

The Reading Ceiling

One of the clearest places the One Step Above theory shows up is in reading.

In many communities, being able to read simply means you can read something, not that you can read deeply.

Kids in high school who can only read at a middle-grade level often spend years mocking those who cannot read at all.

They feel accomplished and superior. So they stop practicing.

They never develop into fluent, analytical, or expansive readers. The ceiling locks in, not because they lack ability, but because comparison replaced curiosity.

Practice Matters More Than Talent

Here's a truth most people never hear: You become good at **whatever you do a lot**.

Not what you think about.

Not what you intend.

What you practice.

If books aren't in the house, reading never becomes natural. If writing isn't modeled, expression never becomes fluid. If learning isn't rewarded, effort disappears. So intelligence gets rerouted.

Other skills turn up:

- mental math
- pattern recognition
- verbal agility
- situational awareness

These are real strengths, but without discipline, they stay unrefined.

When School Becomes the Enemy

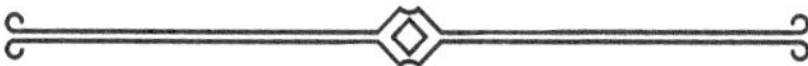

For many people, school doesn't feel like an opportunity. It feels like exposure.

Misspellings get laughed at.

Questions get dismissed.

Mistakes get remembered.

So the mind adapts. Instead of learning, it learns **avoidance**. Instead of curiosity, it chooses confidence. Instead of mastery, it chooses being "better than someone else."

That's One Step Above protecting identity.

Being "Naturally Smart" Is a Trap

People often say:

- ◆ "I'm just not a school person."
- ◆ "I learn differently."
- ◆ "I'm smart, just not like that."

Sometimes that's true. It is often also a shield. Real education eventually humbles everyone.

It requires:

- ◆ repetition
- ◆ correction
- ◆ sitting in confusion
- ◆ being wrong publicly

The One Step Above prison makes those experiences feel humiliating instead of necessary. So people stop short.

Education is Expansion, Not Proof

True education isn't about proving intelligence. It's about **expanding capacity**. Reading until comprehension deepens. Writing until thought sharpens. Learning until confidence no longer needs comparison.

That's why people who return to education later in life often grow faster. They're no longer trying to protect an image. They're trying to understand.

ASK YOURSELF

Did I stop learning because I wasn't capable… Or because I was already "smart enough" where I was?

____

____

____

____

____

____

____

That answer reveals whether education stalled because of a lack or because of a ceiling.

Friend Groups and the Cost of Outgrowing the Room

"Some rooms don't push you forward. They keep you familiar."

—Reginald A. Calloway

Most people don't stop growing because they fail. They stop growing because **they succeed too far ahead of the people they love**.

The Unspoken Contract

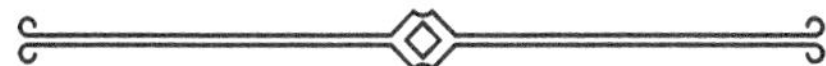

Every friend group has a silent agreement. One that lasts forever. No meeting. No discussion. No vote. Just an understanding.

We can grow, but not so much that it changes who we are.

As long as everyone stays within range, the group feels safe. That range is the ceiling.

How the Group
Maintains Balance

Friend groups don't need rules. They use reactions.
Laughter.

Sarcasm.

Silence.

Tone.

When someone starts changing—reading more, thinking differently, making new choices—the group feels it immediately, and the correction begins. Not harshly; casually.

"You're acting differently."

"You think you're better now."

"You on some other stuff."

Those phrases aren't jokes. They're **signals**.

Why Growth Feels Like Betrayal

When one person grows, the group has to face something uncomfortable:

Growth was possible.

That realization forces comparison. Comparison forces accountability, and accountability threatens comfort.

So instead of confronting their own stagnation, the group reframes the person who's changing.

They don't say, "You've grown."

They say, "You've changed."

That one word turns progress into disloyalty.

The Moment the Room Turns

There's always a moment when you feel it. The energy shifts. The jokes stop landing.

The silence gets longer. The warmth cools.

What used to be curiosity becomes irritation. What used to be support becomes distance. That's the cost of outgrowing the room.

This is when sharing information starts to feel risky. Opportunities get misread as ego. Advice gets heard as judgment. Excitement gets labeled as arrogance.

Not because you're wrong, but because your movement threatens the group's identity. So the group protects itself, and the easiest way to do that is to neutralize you.

How People Shrink Without Noticing

Most people don't leave friend groups dramatically. They **edit themselves**.

They:

- Stop talking about certain things
- downplay wins
- avoid subjects that spark tension

They stay, but smaller. Over time, they forget who they were becoming. This prison is powerful because it uses love as leverage.

It doesn't say, "Don't grow."

It says, "Don't make us uncomfortable."

For people who've already lost a lot, belonging feels more important than expansion, so they choose familiarity over possibility.

The Necessary Shift

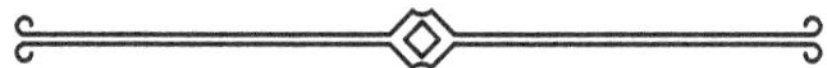

Outgrowing a room doesn't mean abandoning people.

It means changing where you get:

- ◆ validation
- ◆ reflection
- ◆ direction

You stop asking old environments to confirm new versions of you.

That's maturity.

Who do I feel smaller around, and why am I still negotiating my growth there?

Those answers tell you which rooms you've already outgrown.

Families That Enforce Ceilings

"Sometimes the hardest ceiling to break is the one built by people who love you and need you to stay where they learned how to survive."

–Reginald A. Calloway

The hardest ceilings to break aren't built by enemies. They're built by family. Not because families are cruel. But because families are where survival rules are learned first.

Long before the world tells you who you can be, your family teaches you what's acceptable and what is not acceptable. This is not learned through rules, but taught through reactions.

What excites them. What worries them. What they celebrate quietly and what makes the room go silent. By the time you're old enough to dream, you already know which dreams create discomfort. That discomfort is the ceiling.

How Love Becomes a Boundary

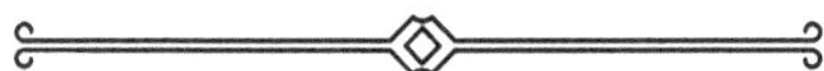

Most families don't believe they are limiting you. They believe they are protecting you.

Protecting you from:

- disappointment
- failure
- embarrassment
- rejection

So when you reach for something unfamiliar, they respond with caution dressed as care:

- "That's not realistic."
- "People like us don't do that."
- "Don't get your hopes up."
- "Be grateful for what you got."

What sounds like wisdom is often fear passed down as guidance.

Role Assignment and Identity Lock

Every family assigns roles.

The responsible one.

The smart one.

The helper.

The rebel.

The disappointment.

These roles help families function. They also quietly define how far you're allowed to grow. Once your role is set, movement becomes suspicious.

If you're the "problem child," success feels temporary.

If you're the "smart one," struggle feels unacceptable.

If you're the "helper," ambition feels selfish.

Families enforce ceilings by keeping you where they know how to relate to you.

The Difference in Wealthy Families

In many poor and middle-class families, growth threatens stability. Change feels risky.

Standing out feels dangerous.

In wealthier families, growth is often expected. Children are raised seeing parents sit in rooms where they are not the most powerful, not the most influential, not the most accomplished. Being smaller is normalized. Exposure is familiar.

When someone in those families enters a bigger room, the message isn't:

"Don't embarrass us."

It's, "Pay attention. Learn how this works."

The ceiling isn't removed because wealth makes people better. It's removed because **being outmatched isn't considered shameful**.

The Language of
the Ceiling

Family ceilings don't sound cruel. They sound familiar.

"You changed."

"Money changed you."

"You don't come around as you used to."

"You too good for us now?"

What they're really saying is: Your growth is changing the story we tell ourselves; and stories feel safer than truth.

Conditional Comfort

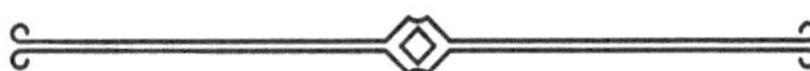

This is the quiet trade many people make without realizing it: They trade potential for peace.

They stay:

- close enough to be loved
- small enough to be understood
- reachable enough to be accepted

And they call it loyalty.

In wealthier environments, loyalty is often framed as expansion, bringing knowledge back, opening doors, and extending opportunity.

In scarcity-shaped families, loyalty is framed as a form of containment.

Don't outgrow us.

Don't leave us behind.

Don't make us uncomfortable.

Why This Ceiling Is So Hard to Break

You can quit a job. You can change cities. You can outgrow friends, but family is different.

Family remembers who you were when you needed them, and sometimes they need you to stay with that version so they won't have to face what they never tried.

That's why this ceiling holds so tightly,

The Way Out (Without Burning Everything Down)

Breaking this ceiling doesn't mean cutting people off. It means ending the negotiation.

You stop explaining your ambition.

You stop justifying your growth.

You stop shrinking to keep the peace.

You let your life speak. You accept that some people can only love you from a distance.

The Truth Most People Avoid

Families don't enforce ceilings because they're malicious. They enforce them because ceilings keep them safe. Breaking one feels like betrayal, even when it's the healthiest thing you can do.

ASK YOURSELF

Are there dreams or goals I have held back from pursuing because I worry about how my family might react or feel about my growth? What are they?

The Guilt Ceiling: Why Growth Starts to Feel Selfish

"Guilt is not a signal to stop. It's a signal that you've outgrown who you were allowed to be."

—Reginald A. Calloway

For many people, the ceiling doesn't collapse when they leave their environment. It follows them. It shows up as **guilt**.

When Progress Triggers Discomfort

At a certain point in growth, something strange happens.

You're no longer struggling.

You're no longer surviving.

You're starting to *build*.

And instead of joy, a quiet discomfort creeps in. You start thinking:

- "Why me?"
- "Do I deserve this?"
- "What about everyone else?"

This isn't humility. It's the guilt ceiling activating.

How Guilt Gets Installed

Guilt usually enters early. It's taught in small moments:

- When you succeed, and others don't
- When you leave, and others stay
- When you change, and others can't

You learn without anyone saying it out loud that growth creates imbalance. An imbalance feels wrong. You internalize a rule:

If I go too far, someone I love will feel left behind.

That rule doesn't stop ambition. It **slows it**.

Why Guilt Feels Like Morality

The most dangerous thing about guilt is that it masquerades as goodness.

It sounds like:

- loyalty
- empathy
- humility
- compassion

But often it's just **unresolved attachment to old identities**.

You're not being kind.

You're being cautious.

You're trying to grow *without outgrowing*. That's impossible.

How People Self-Sabotage Quietly

The guilt ceiling doesn't usually make people quit.

It makes them:

♦ undercharge

♦ overgive

♦ delay decisions

♦ avoid opportunities

♦ stay accessible when they need distance

They keep one foot behind them, just in case.

Just in case someone needs them.

Just in case someone feels abandoned.

Just in case they go "too far."

That hesitation compounds.

Why Success Feels Lonelier Than Failure

Failure invites sympathy. Success invites comparison. Comparison creates silence.

When people start rising, they often feel alone for the first time, not because they have lost people, but because **they can't talk freely anymore**.

That silence turns inward. Guilt fills it.

The Hidden Question Beneath Guilt

Most guilt reduces to one question: *Who am I without the people who needed me?*

If your identity was built on:

- being the helper
- being the strong one
- being the example
- being the survivor

Then success threatens that role.

You don't just grow, you disappear from the identity that kept you safe. That's terrifying.

The Necessary Reframe

Growth is not abandonment. Growth is **expansion**. You are not responsible for managing other people's comfort with your evolution. You are responsible for:

- living honestly
- using your capacity fully
- not shrinking to case tension

Anything less is quite self-betrayal.

How the Guilt
Ceiling Breaks

The guilt ceiling doesn't break through force. It breaks through acceptance.

Acceptance that:

- Not everyone can come with you
- Not everyone will understand
- Not everyone needs access

None of those truths makes you a bad person. They make you **free**.

ASK YOURSELF

Where have I been holding back, not because I couldn't go forward, but because it felt wrong to do so?

____

____

____

____

____

____

____

____

That's where guilt has been negotiating your future.

Entrepreneurs Who Refuse Partnerships, Control Disguised as Independence

"Some entrepreneurs don't fail because they lack opportunity. They fail because they refuse to stop being the biggest thing they've ever built."

–Reginald A. Calloway

There is a moment in almost every entrepreneur's life when effort stops being the problem. **Control** becomes the ceiling.

How Most Entrepreneurs Are Born

ost entrepreneurs don't start with privilege.

They start with:

- distrust
- scarcity
- self-reliance
- necessity

They build alone because they *have* to. That loneliness becomes a badge of honor.

"I did this myself."

"I don't need anybody."

"I built this from the ground up."

At first, that identity saves you. Later, it traps you.

When Growth Requires Letting Go

At a certain point, growth stops responding to hustle. It demands:

- ♦ capital
- ♦ systems
- ♦ delegation
- ♦ collaboration

That's where the internal conflict begins

Because now the question isn't, *"Can I build this?"*

It's, *"Can I stop being the center of it?"*

For people shaped by One Step Above, that feels like loss.

Why Partnerships Feel Dangerous

Partnerships don't just require trust. They require **shared authority**.

They force you to:

- be challenged
- be corrected
- be outpaced
- be absorbed into something bigger

If your identity was built on being "the one who made it," then walking into a room where you're no longer special feels like erasure, even if the outcome is expansion.

So entrepreneurs avoid it. Not consciously; instinctively.

"I Don't Want Nobody in My Business"

This sentence sounds like wisdom. Most of the time, it's fear.

Fear of:

- losing control
- being exposed
- being replaced
- being overshadowed

So instead of partners, entrepreneurs hire:

- Employees they can dominate
- vendors they can replace
- help without power

The business grows, only as far as the owner's nervous system allows. That's the ceiling.

The One Step
Above Trade-Off

One Step Above entrepreneurs often choose:

- 100% ownership of something small
- over 20% ownership of something massive

The math doesn't matter. Identity does. Being *"Above"* feels safer than being *inside* something larger. So scale stays theoretical.

How Integrity Gets Used as Armor

This prison hides behind values.

"I'm protecting my vision."

"I won't compromise."

"I want to stay true."

Sometimes that's real. Often, it's just **identity preservation** disguised as principle.

Real integrity asks, "*What serves the mission best?*"

One Step Above asks, "*How do I stay in control?*"

Why the Business Can't Outgrow the Person

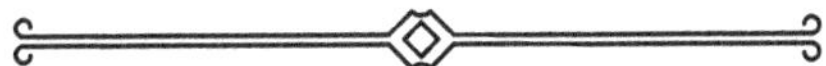

When control is the priority, the business becomes dependent on the founder.

Decisions bottleneck.

Energy drains.

Growth plateaus.

Eventually, the entrepreneur feels exhausted, not because they're doing too much, but because **they're doing everything**. That's not leadership. That's containment.

The Exit

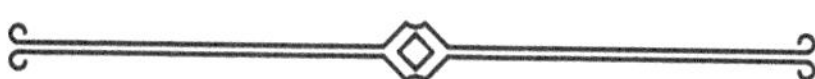

Leaving this version of the prison doesn't mean saying yes to everyone. It means learning how to sit in rooms where:

- ♦ You don't dominate
- ♦ You don't control the pace
- ♦ You don't get the final word

And staying grounded anyway. That's when scale becomes possible.

ASK YOURSELF

Am I avoiding this partnership because it's wrong... Or because it would make me ordinary again?

That answer tells the truth.

SECTION EIGHT

Why Humility Gets Weaponized

Humility is a virtue, but when it's used to limit growth, it stops being humility and becomes control.

–Reginald A. Calloway

Humility is supposed to be grounding. In many environments, it becomes a leash.

When Humility Stops Being a Virtue

True humility sounds like:

- openness
- curiosity
- willingness to learn

Weaponized humility sounds like:

- "Stay in your place."
- "Don't do too much."
- "Don't get beside yourself."

It doesn't tell you to be humble. It tells you to **stay small**.

How Humility Becomes Social Control

In One Step Above environments, humility gets redefined.

It no longer means: *I don't know everything.*

It means: *I won't threaten anyone.*

So ambition gets framed as arrogance. Confidence gets framed as ego. Growth gets framed as disrespect. Not because it is, but because it disrupts the hierarchy.

"Don't Forget Where You Came From"

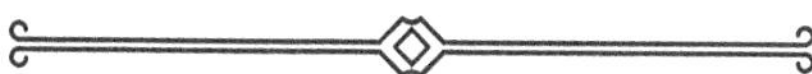

This phrase sounds like wisdom. Often it's used as a ceiling.

It doesn't mean "Honor your roots."

It means: *Don't outgrow them.*

So people learn to apologize for success, to downplay wins, and to explain progress. Humility becomes performance.

Why This Works So Well

Weaponized humility is effective because it uses **morality** to enforce limits.

You're not told, "Stop growing."

You're told, "Be a good person."

And no one wants to feel like growth makes them bad, so people shrink quietly and call it character.

The Difference Between Humility and Submission

Real humility says, "*I can learn from anyone.*" Weaponized humility says, "*I shouldn't surpass anyone.*"

One leads to expansion. The other leads to containment.

ASK YOURSELF

Am I being humble, or am I being managed?

SECTION NINE

Leaving the Ceiling Without Burning the World Down

"Growth doesn't require destruction. It requires clarity."

–Reginald A. Calloway

Seeing the ceiling changes everything. Leaving it requires care.

Why People Stay Even After They See It

Most people don't stay because they're unaware of it. They stay because leaving feels destructive.

They fear:

- losing relationships
- being misunderstood
- being labeled selfish
- becoming isolated

So they hesitate.

The Myth of the
Dramatic Exit

Leaving the One Step Above ceiling does **not** require:

- cutting everyone off
- announcing your growth
- proving anything
- making enemies

That's ego. Real departure is quieter.

You stop:

- explaining yourself
- shrinking to fit rooms
- seeking approval from old mirrors

You start:

- choosing environments intentionally
- letting silence replace argument
- allowing distance without resentment

You don't burn bridges. You **outgrow dependence on them**.

Boundaries Without Hostility

Boundaries don't need speeches.

They show up as:

- ♦ different choices
- ♦ different rhythms
- ♦ different standards

Some people will adjust. Some won't. Both outcomes are okay.

The Loneliness Phase

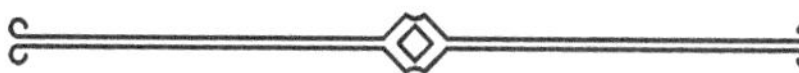

There is usually a quiet stretch after leaving. Not loneliness from rejection, but from **reorientation**.
Old rooms don't fit.
New rooms aren't familiar yet.
This is normal. Don't turn back here.

The Reframe That Keeps You Grounded

You are not leaving people behind. You are leaving **limitations** behind.

People can join you at any time.

ASK YOURSELF

Am I trying to prove my growth to others, or am I quietly making the choices that move my life forward?

Becoming Comfortable Being a Beginner Again

"The ceiling doesn't break when you fight it. It breaks when you outgrow the need to stand above anyone at all."

–Reginald A. Calloway

Every ceiling breaks the same way. You become a beginner on purpose.

Why Beginners
Feel Unsafe

Being a beginner means:

    ♦ not knowing

    ♦ asking questions

    ♦ being corrected

    ♦ looking slow

For someone raised in One Step Above, this feels unbearable. Because superiority once kept you safe.

Why Mastery Always Starts Here

Every expert was once:

- awkward
- confused
- unsure

They didn't avoid that stage. They **stayed in it**. That's the difference.

The Real Work
of Growth

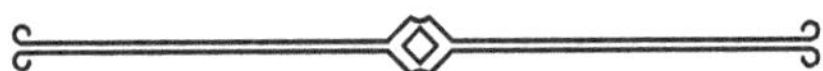

Growth isn't confidence. It's tolerance for discomfort.

The willingness to:

- sit in rooms where you're not special
- learn from people younger than you
- be corrected without collapsing

That's not a weakness. That's expansion.

The Final Ceiling

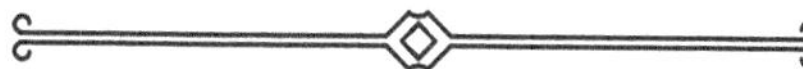

Most people would rather be impressive in a small room than invisible in a larger one but only the second leads to transformation.

When you accept this, you stop needing:

- comparison
- hierarchy
- validation

You start seeking:

- depth
- skill
- truth

And suddenly, the ceiling loses its grip.

ASK YOURSELF

Where am I still choosing familiarity over growth because being a beginner scares me more than staying limited?

____

____

____

____

____

____

____

____

That's where your next expansion lives.

Epilogue: Beyond One Step Above

By the time you reach the end of this book, you may notice something subtle. The world hasn't changed. The way you look at it might have. That's enough.

The goal of this book was never to convince you to abandon your life, your people, or your past. It was to help you recognize where growth may have quietly slowed, not because you failed, but because you adapted.

Being one step ahead often starts as a matter of survival. It becomes a ceiling only when it's mistaken for the destination.

If this book has done its job, you may now see moments—past or present—where you chose familiarity over expansion, safety over curiosity, position over possibility. That recognition isn't meant to bring regret.

It's meant to bring **choice**.

You don't have to leave everything behind to grow.

You don't have to announce your evolution.

You don't have to prove anything to anyone.

Sometimes growth is simply allowing yourself to learn again.

To be new at something.

To sit in rooms where you don't stand out.

To let go of the need to be above in order to be okay.

That's not loss.

That's freedom.

If you take only one thing from this book, let it be this:

Growth doesn't require superiority. It requires openness. The moment you stop needing to be one step above, is the moment the ceiling disappears.